★ *A Gone-to-Texas Dual Biography*

Moses Austin
and
Stephen F. Austin

Thanks to Dr. David Gracy for sharing his
knowledge of Moses Austin
and
to all those whose labors brought this
book into being.

G.T.T.

During the 1800s, many families in Southern states
left their homes hoping to find land and prosperity in
Texas. On the doors of their deserted houses, they
scrawled the letters G.T.T. This is how they let their
neighbors know that they had

Gone-To-Texas.

★ *A Gone-to-Texas Dual Biography*

Moses Austin
and
Stephen F. Austin

by Betsy Warren

Hendrick-Long Publishing Co.
DALLAS

Library of Congress Cataloging-in-Publication Data

Warren, Betsy.
    Moses Austin and Stephen F. Austin: a gone to Texas dual
    biography/Betsy Warren.
        p. cm.
    Includes bibliographical references and index.
    ISBN 0-937460-96-6 (hc)
    1. Austin, Moses, 1761-1821. 2. Austin, Stephen F. (Stephen
Fuller), 1793-1836. 3. Pioneers—Texas—Biography. 4. Texas—
History—To 1846—Biography. I. Title.
F389.W35 1995   95-13875
976.4'02'0922—dc20   CIP
[B]

ISBN 0-937460-96-6
© 1996 Betsy Warren
Hendrick-Long Publishing Co.
P.O. Box 25123
Dallas, Texas 75225

iv

Contents

INTRODUCTION

Moses Austin
1761–1821

Stephen Fuller Austin
1793–1836

This is the true story of a father and his son. Their names were Moses and Stephen F. Austin.

Many difficulties, dangers, and lonely times filled the lives of Moses and his son. But they were brave and good men who worked hard all the days of their lives.

Because it opened the way for much of the settlement of western America, the work of Moses and Stephen F. Austin was important to Texas and to all of America as well.

Chapter 1

FAMILY ROOTS

Families named Austin came from England to America in the year 1638. American colonies were ruled by England. The Austins settled at Boston in the Colony of Massachusetts.

In later years, some members of the Austin family moved to western Massachusetts, which eventually became the Colony of Connecticut.

1638

Birthplace of Moses Austin

1761   Moses Austin was born in the town of Durham, Connecticut, in the year 1761.

    The parents of Moses—Elias and Eunice—died when Moses was a young boy. He went to Middletown, Connecticut, to live with his married sister and to work in her husband's store.

1783   When Moses was 22, he moved to Philadelphia. With two partners, he ran a dry-goods store. When they opened several more stores, Moses was chosen to start a new one in Richmond, Virginia.

1785   Moses Austin married Maria Brown, the daughter of a New Jersey businessman. They moved to Rich-mond and had a fine brick house with six servants to help them.

Maria Brown Austin
1768–1824

By this time, England no longer ruled the American colonies. The Thirteen Colonies had become the United States of America. George Washington became the first president of the United States in 1789. His home was in Virginia at Mount Vernon.

George Washington's home – Mount Vernon, Virginia

When Moses Austin bought some lead mines in southwestern Virginia, he and Maria moved there. Moses hired many workers, improved the mines, and found new markets for the lead. It was dug from the ground to be made into bowls, bullets, and metal roofing.

Moses also was the owner of a surveying company and was captain of the Wythe County militia.

1793   The village that grew up around the lead mines was called Austinville. Here, Moses and Maria had their first son ... Stephen Fuller Austin. Two years later, his little sister, Emily, was born in the Austinville home.

Moses was happy with his family and with the lead mining business. At first, the mines prospered and so did the store back in Richmond.

However, three years later, the lead mining business was not doing well. Moses became restless. He wanted to find a place where there would be greater deposits of lead to be mined.

Richmond, Virginia, 1796

4

Chapter 2

A TRIP TO THE WEST

When Stephen was three years old, his father heard about vast deposits of lead far to the west. Moses wanted to go see where the lead was. He knew it was in the Spanish-held territory of Missouri.

With a friend, Josiah Bell, Moses made a trip on horseback to southeastern Missouri. They traveled during a bitterly cold December. Rivers and streams were frozen over. The horses floundered in snow that was two feet deep. It was many miles between the few settlements in the lonely wilderness. Moses and Josiah once were

1796

lost for five days. Along with their animals, they suffered from cold and hunger.

At last, the men crossed the Mississippi River at St. Louis. Two hundred houses were in the town, but there were no inns where travelers could stay.

St. Louis riverfront in early days

Moses and Josiah soon left St. Louis. They went 60 miles south to Ste. Genevieve, a small village on the Mississippi River.

At one time, the land west of the Mississippi had belonged to France. But now it belonged to Spain. However, the commandant of Ste. Genevieve was a Frenchman—François Valle. He welcomed the men and lent Moses a carriage drawn by two horses.

With John Jones, a new friend, Moses drove 30 miles west to the land where the lead was. It took two days. The men found 40 acres of huge lead deposits near Breton Creek. The place was called by a French name, Mine à Breton. A great deal of lead lay on top of the ground, and much more was only three feet below.

Moses saw that it would not be difficult to dig up the lead. To carry the heavy loads over rough hills to Ste. Genevieve would be the hardest part of the work. But then it could be shipped down the Mississippi on barges, across the Gulf of Mexico, and on to markets in the United States and foreign countries.

With several partners, Moses immediately applied for the grant of a league of land that held the lead. Then, he hurried back to Virginia to gather his family and workmen together for the move to Missouri.

By the time Moses and Josiah reached home in Austinville, they had traveled 2,000 miles.

River landing at Ste. Genevieve in 1785

Chapter 3

MOVING TO MISSOURI TERRITORY

1798   Forty people prepared for the trip to Missouri— the Austin family, servants, drivers, and work- men. Nine wagons were loaded with baggage and furniture. The Austins rode in a coach pulled by four strong horses.

At the Kanawha River, the travelers and all the baggage went on long barges. The barges

Meeting of the Kanawha and Ohio rivers

A barge on the Ohio River in the early 1800s

floated down the Kanawha and Ohio rivers, then
up the Mississippi to Ste. Genevieve. The trip
lasted three months.

Although it was the first town to be settled west
of the Mississippi, Ste. Genevieve had only 100
houses. Most of the people were French or Spanish
hunters and traders. Osage Indians roamed in the
surrounding hills and were often a threat to the
settlers.

Leaving his family in a cabin in the town for
safety, Moses hurried to Mine à Breton. He hired
150 men to dig the lead from the ground. Then he

Lead mining in early times

and his workmen built a saw-mill, a flour mill, furnaces for melting lead, and a company store.

For his family, Moses built a large house. He called it Durham Hall after his birthplace in Durham, Connecticut.

1801   Moses worked to develop the mines and to find markets where the lead could be sold. In 1801, he traveled 2,000 miles. With two flatboats loaded

Ash furnace used for melting lead

Durham Hall standing above Breton Creek

with lead, he went down the Mississippi hoping
to find buyers in New Orleans. He also wanted to
ask the Spanish government to complete his land
grant. However, the Spanish officials were busy
selling the lands of Arkansas and Missouri to the
United States. They were not able to help Moses
with the grant.

Although he was discouraged, Moses
managed to sell the lead. After buying supplies
for the mines and his store, he loaded them on
the flatboats and went back up the river. At Ste.
Genevieve, he put the supplies in wagons and
carted them home to Mine à Breton.

Chapter 4

INDIAN ATTACK

1802

The Osage Indians were angry because Moses had brought new settlers into their hunting territory. One time, 30 Indians surrounded Durham Hall. They were shooting arrows and yelling loud war whoops. From the house, Moses and nine of his workmen shot at the Indians. Young Stephen had helped carry buckets of sand to put by the windows. The sand would be used to put out fires if the Indians shot flaming arrows into the house.

Osage Indians

It was a frightening time for everyone. But after a while, the Indians left. They did not come back again. That night, Moses wrote in the family Bible about the Indian attack. This is the reason we know about it.

Chapter 5

SCHOOL DAYS

Another boy was born to the Austins in 1803. They named him James Brown Austin and called him "Brown."

In 1804, Moses was chosen to be a judge in the Ste. Genevieve District. In the same year, he sent Stephen to Connecticut to go to school. With an older cousin, the 11-year-old boy traveled 1,000 miles on river boats going to the East.

Stephen entered Bacon Academy in Colchester, Connecticut. He did well in his studies and made friendships easily. On holidays, he visited relatives of the Austin family who lived in that area. Also, he had a miniature portrait painted of himself and sent it home to his family.

Stephen stayed three years at Bacon Academy. He wrote often to his family. His father answered with long

Stephen Austin
age 11

Bacon Academy in Colchester, Connecticut

letters encouraging him to work hard in his studies.
Moses was eager for his son to be well educated,
and Stephen was just as eager to please his father.

After graduating, Stephen crossed the
Allegheny Mountains in a stagecoach to enter
Transylvania University in Lexington, Kentucky. It
was the only university in the West, and it was
gaining a fine reputation.

Stephen studied mathematics, geography,
astronomy, philosophy, history, and music. He
played the flute to accompany singing societies and
enjoyed dancing at parties. Best of all, he was able
to visit with his sister, Emily, who was in boarding
school in Lexington. It was the first time in four
years that Stephen had seen a member of his family.

Chapter 6

STEPHEN GOES HOME

After only one year at the university, Stephen was called home. The mining business was not doing well, and Moses needed his son's help. Besides, it was time for Emily and Brown to have their turn at school in the East.

1810

Back in Mine à Breton, Stephen kept the account books for the lead mines and worked in the company store. He sold hardware and household furnishings which were shipped in from the Eastern states.

Stephen became well acquainted with hunters, miners, Indians, and travelers who came into the store. He learned to get along with all types of people and to treat them with respect.

In May, 1812, Moses asked Stephen to take a barge of lead down the Mississippi to New

A flatboat floating from St. Louis to New Orleans

Orleans, a four-month trip. The lead was to be taken across the Gulf of Mexico and on to New York to be sold. But, near New Orleans, the barge had an accident. It sank to the bottom of the river. Experienced rivermen told Stephen that the lead cargo was too heavy to be raised from the river bottom. But Stephen did not give up. Patiently, he waited until the river waters lowered. Then, with many helpers, he raised the barge of lead and started down the river once more.

When he reached New Orleans, Stephen heard that the United States had gone to war with England. If he went into the Gulf of Mexico, English ships would capture his barge and use the lead for making bullets to be used against the Americans. So, Stephen found American buyers in New Orleans. He sold the lead to them and returned safely home many months later.

Chapter 7

HARD TIMES

In 1813, Emily married James Bryan, a merchant in Mine à Breton. They moved to nearby Hazel Run, a small community that had grown around lead mines and stores that James Bryan owned. It was close to Ste. Genevieve.

Although the United States had won the war against England, it was harder and harder for people to make a living. No one could find jobs. Farmers lost their lands because they had no money to buy tools and seeds or to pay their debts. Moses could not collect money that was owed to him, and he could not pay back the loans that banks had given to him.

Trying to save expenses by moving closer to the river, Moses had bought property at Joachim Creek where it emptied into the Mississippi. Barges and boats could land at the river shore to pick up shipments of lead.

The Austin house by the river at Herculaneum, Missouri

Moses also built a home and stores at the village he called Herculaneum. Soon, several Austin relatives came from Connecticut to start businesses in Herculaneum. The most successful was a leather tanning factory.

On top of a nearby cliff, Moses built a "shot tower." Molten lead was dropped through a sieve from the top of the tower. The hot pieces of lead hardened into ball shapes as they fell into a tank of water far below. Moses found a few markets for the bullets and other lead products in the eastern

United States, but it was becoming harder and harder to make a profit.

1814

In 1814, the people of Mine à Breton changed the name of their town to Potosi. Men in the town tried to think of ways to make jobs available. Moses and the townsmen built a fine large building for a courthouse in Potosi. They hoped that it would attract business and more people to their area.

Courthouse is the large building at top right. Potosi (1818)

Chapter 8

TIMES GROW WORSE

1816   Trying to find ways to help people get loans, Moses and several partners started a bank in St. Louis. But the hard times were growing worse. When the bank failed three years later, Moses became desperate. He was in danger of losing all of his properties because he could not pay back the money he had borrowed.

Stephen thought he could help his family by entering public affairs. In 1814, he won an election to the legislature of the Missouri Territory which met in St. Louis. During almost six years in the legislature, he became keenly interested in the process of making laws.

1819   When the United States opened the Territory of Arkansas for settlers, Stephen planned to develop land on the site of present-day Little Rock. Writing articles for newspapers, he urged settlers to come into Arkansas. When they did not come, Stephen went to New Orleans. He began the study of law with Judge Joseph H. Hawkins, the brother of a friend.

Chapter 9

MOSES RIDES TO TEXAS

For 300 years, the Spanish had owned the area of Texas. It was an immense wilderness filled with Indians who fought intruders. To get help in protecting their lands, Spain offered to give land free to anyone who would come to Texas to build homes and towns. Spain expected settlers to become Spanish citizens, to be baptized as Catholics, and to act as buffers against Indians and outsiders.

1820

When Moses Austin heard of this offer, he saw that it was an opportunity for families in the United States to build new lives and have a better future. He made plans to go see the Spanish governor in San Antonio, Texas. He hoped to gain permission from Governor Antonio Martínez to make colonies in Texas.

1820   In the fall of 1820, Moses left Potosi for Arkansas. After a visit with Stephen in Little Rock in November, he headed for San Antonio on a grey horse. Richmond, a young servant, also rode with him.

A month later when they arrived in San Antonio, Governor Martínez refused to listen to Moses' plan to bring colonists into Texas. He even demanded that Moses get out of the city by nightfall. The Sr niards had changed their minds.

They decided that they did not want people from the United States to come into their country. They were afraid that the Americans might take Texas away from them.

Greatly discouraged, Moses prepared to leave. But as he walked across Military Plaza, a man came running to greet him. It was Baron de Bastrop, a friend he had not seen for many years!

Spanish governor's palace built in 1749

When Moses told him what had happened, Bastrop said, "The governor is a friend of mine. I know that when I tell him you have been a respected Spanish citizen in Missouri, he will talk to you."

Three days later, Moses met with Governor Martínez, who gave permission for Moses to bring 300 families from the United States to make homes. He promised to send officials to help Moses pick out 200,000 acres of land in East Texas for his colony.

With joy, Moses and Richmond started back to Missouri to gather colonists for Texas. Since it was safer for several men to travel together because of hostile Indians, Moses agreed to let a man named Jacob Kirkham go with them.

After riding several days, the men camped one night near the Trinity River. While Moses and Richmond slept, Kirkham stole away with their horses and provisions.

That same night, a panther jumped from a tree, landing on Moses as he slept. Only the thick buffalo robe that covered Moses kept him from harm. He shouted and shook the robe, scaring the panther away.

When Moses and Richmond realized that their food, supplies, and horses were gone, they began walking to the northeast. For eight days, the men walked through the lonely wilderness. They had nothing to eat except a few berries and roots that they found. When they finally reached the trading post of Hugh McGuffin near the Sabine River, both men were ill and starving. The McGuffins took them into their home and cared for them.

Three weeks later, although he was still very ill, Moses insisted on leaving for Missouri. Richmond was too sick to go along and had to be left with the McGuffins.

Going by boat down the Red River and then 1821 up the Mississippi, Moses reached home safely. Maria and Emily begged him to rest so he could get completely well. Yet, he immediately began to travel around the countryside to gather families and workmen for the move to Texas. Also, he had to sell all of his properties to pay debts that were owed on the lead mines. By now, Moses was almost penniless.

In June, while on his way to Potosi, Moses stopped to see his daughter Emily at her home in Hazel Run. He was so ill he had to be helped from his horse and carried to the house.

A few days later, Moses knew that he would not live much longer. He asked his wife, Maria, to

write a letter to their son Stephen in New Orleans.
It was to be one of the most fateful letters ever
written. It also held Moses' last words to his son
Stephen.

Chapter 10

IN HIS FATHER'S FOOTSTEPS

In New Orleans, Stephen received the letter from his father and mother. Here is a part of the letter written by his mother:

> "He called me to his bedside and with much distress and difficulty of speech begged me to tell you to take his place, and if God in his wisdom thought best to disappoint him in the accomplishment of his wishes and plans formed for the benefit of his family, he prayed him to extend His goodness to you and enable you to go on with the business in the same way he would have done had not sickness and ... death prevented him."

This letter changed the course of Stephen's life. It also determined the future of Texas.

Stephen knew how hard his father had worked to take care of his family. And even though he liked studying law, he wanted to fulfill his father's hopes and plans. Putting on his

buckskin clothes, he started for Texas with two pistols, a tomahawk, and a horse. Making rafts of saplings tied together with grapevines, he crossed rivers and creeks along the way, his horse swimming alongside. Since he passed through only two small villages, he had to find his own food in the fields and forests and streams. Deer, fish, rabbits, and turtles kept him well supplied.

Chapter 11

San Antonio, 1840

A NEW LIFE IN TEXAS

Spanish officials met Stephen in San Antonio. They went with him to help him pick out 200,000 acres in East Texas for the colony. For three months, they explored the land between the Brazos and Colorado rivers. When Stephen saw how beautiful it was, he began to get enthusiastic about a new life in Texas.

It was not hard to find people who wanted to move to Texas. Soon, there were 300 families from the United States settling on the land grant. They dug wells, ran a ferry over the Brazos, built log cabins for homes and

Ferry boat

29

shops, and began to raise crops and cattle. The settlers called their village San Felipe de Austin.

Just as the colony was getting started, Mexico won its freedom from Spain after 10 years of rebellion. The new Mexican officials informed Stephen he would have to go to Mexico City to establish his rights to the land.

"The land grant was given by Spain to your father, not to you," they said. "And now *Mexico* must approve the grant for you."

Flag of Mexico

With two companions, Stephen started on the long trip south to Mexico. Near the Nueces River, the three men were captured by 50 Comanche Indians who thought they were Spaniards and took away all their possessions. When Stephen finally convinced the Indians that they were friendly Americans, the Comanches gave everything back except four blankets, a bridle, and a Spanish grammar book.

Stephen continued the journey alone. For safety from robbers, he dressed in disguise

Comanche warrior

Main Plaza in Mexico City

as a poor farm workman while he rode the 1,200 miles to Mexico City.

Stephen was impressed with the beauty of the city which was the capital for both Mexico and Texas. He met with a committee to discuss land ownership and laws for his colony. But when a new leader was chosen for Mexico there was great confusion in the city. No one had time to talk further with Stephen.

While waiting for many months to see the officials again, Stephen ran out of money. He had to sell his watch and borrow money in order to buy food. But he spent his time learning the Spanish language and making friends. The

Mexican people liked and trusted him. They invited him to parties and into their homes.

At last, he met again with the Mexican officials. They were pleased that Stephen had learned their language and that he had shown such great patience during the long wait. His land grant was confirmed with 4,428 acres of land being allowed to each family for ranching and 177 acres for farming. Also, Stephen was given the titles of Empresario (land agent) and Colonel, a military title.

1824

More than a year had passed by the time Stephen arrived home in San Felipe. During his absence, Indians had burned settlers' crops and stolen much of their livestock. Many families became so discouraged that they had gone back to their old homes in the United States.

When Stephen learned of the colonists' troubles, he met with the Indian chiefs and made peace treaties with them. Then he brought seeds and tools from San Antonio to give to the remaining colonists.

To make the colonists feel more secure, Stephen made laws that would help in settling disputes. He wrote deeds for land ownership and hired able men to make surveys for the new land grants. Traveling over the area, he drew maps of bays and rivers. He also encouraged the people to build sawmills, cotton gins, and schools. When the Mexican legislature met in Saltillo, he traveled there. Attending its meetings, he tried to bring attention to the problems of Texas.

In spite of being weary from constant overwork, Stephen was a patient, tolerant, and kindly man who put the welfare of his colonists before everything else in his life.

Lonely for his family, Stephen was especially happy when his brother, Brown, came in 1824 to live in Texas. Brown went into Mexico and bought 300 horses with which he started the first stock ranch in the new colony.

During the first seven years of the Austin Colony, 30,000 Americans came to live in Texas. By 1830, there were 4,000 people living in the thriving town of San Felipe. Colonists prospered by raising crops and cattle and selling pelts and cotton to the United States and Mexico. In the town, they built more shops, started newspapers, and held school and church meetings in their homes.

Stephen Austin and other empresarios were granted more land for new colonies. Stephen's new grant spread as far west as the Colorado River in Central Texas.

Colonists going to Texas

Chapter 12

STEPHEN'S FAMILY

Stephen Austin

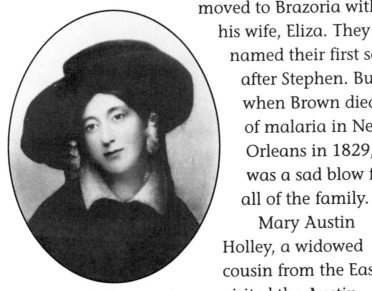

Mary Austin Holley wrote the first book in English about Texas.

In San Felipe, Stephen had very little time to enjoy homelife. He often wished that his relatives would move to Texas. His brother, Brown, who had come from Missouri in 1824, married and moved to Brazoria with his wife, Eliza. They named their first son after Stephen. But when Brown died of malaria in New Orleans in 1829, it was a sad blow for all of the family.

Mary Austin Holley, a widowed cousin from the East, visited the Austin Colony several times.

With great enthusiasm, she wrote books and articles about Texas that were widely read in the United States. Stephen often wrote long letters to her, and it is thought that they planned to be married. But this did not happen.

Peach Point Plantation at Brazoria

Back in Missouri, Maria Austin and Emily's husband, James Bryan, both died in 1824. To support her children, Emily worked as a teacher and took boarders into her home. After Emily married James Perry in 1826, they moved with the children to the Austin Colony, much to Stephen's delight. The Perrys ran a plantation at Peach Point near Brazoria. They saved two rooms at one end of their house for Stephen so he would have a place to work and rest when he came for visits. He always came laden with plants and seeds for Emily's garden and gifts for the children. These were happy times for all the family.

Henry Austin, a cousin, moved from New York to Texas. He was a great help to Stephen in managing business affairs of the colony. A few more relatives also came to Texas at a later time.

Henry Austin

Chapter 13

IN A MEXICAN PRISON

Texas colonists were frustrated with Mexican
rule. They did not like it when Mexico made
them pay taxes but would not let them take part
in making laws. It made them angry when
Mexico took away their guns and ordered that no
more colonists could come from the United States
into Texas.

1832

In 1832, leaders of the colony met in San
Felipe. They asked Stephen to go to the Mexico
City capital to ask for Texas to be an independent
state of Mexico. He agreed to go but begged the
colonists to be patient while he was gone. He
believed that they should obey Mexican laws
until changes could be made peaceably.

1833

In 1833 Stephen made the long trip to Mexico
City. At first, he could not see the officials because
43,000 people in the city were ill with cholera
and many were dying. Stephen became ill, too.
When he recovered and met with officials, they

promised to make better laws for Texas. Then, in December, Stephen left for home.

To his astonishment, Stephen was arrested when he arrived in Saltillo. Guards took him in a coach back to Mexico City and put him in a tiny jail cell. It had no heat and only a straw pallet on the floor. Stephen had to pay a guard to bring food and books to him. Later, he said that in prison he preferred to "have bread and water with books to the best of eating without them." (His only friend was a tiny mouse who shared the cell with him.)

For many months, Stephen did not know just why he had been put in prison. He was not allowed to talk with anyone and was moved several times to different prisons. With each move, he carried along a small black notebook and a pencil stub that he had hidden under his shirt. As often as he could, Stephen wrote in the notebook about his experiences and the feelings of being forgotten. But he also wrote of his plans for the future of Texas.

1835 After nine months, two friends who had come from San Felipe were permitted to see him. During a joyful reunion with Peter Grayson and Spencer Jack, Stephen learned why he had been held. Mexican leaders thought he was urging the Texas colonists to fight for their freedom, and they considered him a traitor.

However, in July, 1835, an order was given by the Mexican president to pardon all political prisoners. After being held for a year in prison and six months under house arrest, Stephen was at last released and allowed to go back to Texas.

Chapter 14

WAR TALK

More than two years had passed by the time Stephen returned by ship to Texas. Great crowds of people met him at the port of Velasco. Some men had ridden all night through the rain to get there in time to greet him. They all wanted to show their respect and appreciation for his

1835

Mexican soldiers

faithfulness to them. After such a long time of feeling lonely and forgotten, Stephen was pleased and heartened by their gratitude.

However, the colonists were talking angrily about fighting Mexico to gain more rights. Stephen tried to keep peace. He reminded them of promises they had made to be loyal Mexican citizens when they had been given their land. But, when Mexico sent soldiers to take away the colonists' guns and to force them to pay taxes, Stephen agreed that Texas must fight.

Chapter 15

TEXANS REBEL
AGAINST MEXICO

The colonists chose Stephen to be head of their volunteer army. This was not to his liking for he was not a military man. However, he led successful skirmishes against Mexican soldiers at Mission Concepción in San Antonio. A short time later, Sam Houston accepted the leadership of the army of Texas, so Stephen was relieved of military duties.

1835

Mission Concepción

General Houston immediately asked Stephen and two other men to go to the United States to borrow money. It would be used to pay soldiers and to buy ammunition. As payment for the loans, the lenders would be given land in Texas.

Near Christmas time, Stephen and the two men went to New Orleans, New York, and Washington. They talked to business leaders and told them how important it was for Texas to win its freedom from Mexico. They were successful in borrowing money that helped the little Texas army to survive.

The Alamo at San Antonio

While Stephen was gone, General Antonio Lopez de Santa Anna, leader of a large Mexican army, marched into Texas. Two battles took place between the Mexicans and Texans. One was at Goliad, and the other at the Alamo in San Antonio.

While on his way with a few soldiers to help at the Alamo, General Houston heard that the Texas men had lost both battles. He knew that his small army was not ready to fight Santa Anna's men, so he led his soldiers in a retreat toward the coast. On the way he tried to train them to be better soldiers.

General Antonio Lopez de Santa Anna

1836

For six weeks, the Texans hid from Santa Anna. General Houston ordered his men to burn the towns of Gonzales and San Felipe as they passed through. He did not want the Mexican army to be able to use the houses or the food stored in them. All the townspeople had fled in fear of Santa Anna's approaching army. Stephen Austin's home was burned to the ground. Nothing but ashes was left of the town of San Felipe.

Chapter 16

VICTORY AT SAN JACINTO

1836

In April, 1836, Santa Anna's army marched to a grassy plain near the coast. Making camp by the San Jacinto River, the Mexicans waited for more troops that were coming to join them. They did not believe that the Texans would fight, because Mexican soldiers greatly outnumbered the Texans.

General Sam Houston

General Houston learned from his scouts where the Mexican troops were. They had set up camp on a grassy field surrounded on three sides by swamps and rivers. The only way across the river was by means of Vince's Bridge. General Houston quickly moved his army over the bridge. Then he ordered his scouts to burn the bridge so that no one could escape over it. After lining up 85 men on horseback to block the only other way to escape from the battlefield, Houston and the Texans were ready to do battle.

At last, on April 21, 1836, the Texan army surprised the Mexicans as they were napping in their tents at San Jacinto. Shouting "Remember Goliad!" and "Remember the Alamo!" the Texans won the battle in less than 20 minutes. Santa Anna was captured as he tried to escape. Texas independence was assured.

On June 27, 1836, Stephen returned home. Learning of the Texas victory, he hoped that now he could retire from public service. He planned to build a home and farm on land near Emily and her family. But Texans wanted him to help them plan a new, strong government.

Chapter 17

PEACE COMES

1836   After winning the war, Texas became a republic. As a country all by itself, it was able to set up its own government and make its own laws. But, first, the people had to choose a president. They also had to elect men to serve as senators and representatives in a legislature.

The first capitol of the Republic of Texas, at Columbia

When the legislature wrote the laws, the people of the Republic of Texas would vote whether to accept them or not.

Sam Houston was elected president of the republic. The town of Columbia was chosen to be the capital where the legislature would meet. President Houston appointed Stephen Austin to be secretary of state for the new republic. He knew that Stephen was the person who best understood how to resolve differences between Texas, Mexico, and the United States.

Although he was ill with malaria, Stephen immediately began to write letters to ask the Americans to allow Texas to become part of the United States. He and many of the leaders believed that Mexico would try again to conquer Texas. They knew that the newly born republic would not be able to stand alone.

Borrowing a two-room cabin from a friend in Columbia, Stephen worked day after day during a chilly December. Each day visitors crowded in to talk with him about how Texas should be governed. Becoming very tired and weak, Stephen lay on a pallet by the fireplace in his workroom. When Emily heard that he was ill with pneumonia, she sent her husband and a son to be with him. Arriving two days after Christmas, they tried to make him comfortable with fresh clothing and warm blankets while they sent for a doctor. But the doctor could not help.

Stephen had no strength left, and he died before the day was over. He was buried on his sister's plantation at Peach Point.

The people of Texas mourned for Stephen because they knew he had given many years of his energy and devotion to make better lives for them. They honored Stephen F. Austin by calling him:

THE FATHER OF TEXAS.

S. F. Austin

NOTES FROM THE AUTHOR

1. A tomahawk, two pistols, and a powder horn that belonged to Stephen are in museums in Austin, Texas.

   Some furniture and a few possessions of the Austins are in remaining rooms of the Perry homestead at Peach Point near Brazoria, Texas.

2. Here are some words written by the Austins. In a letter to his schoolboy son, Moses wrote:

   > ... It's small things that stamp the disposition and temper of a man, and many times Boys lessen their greatness in life by small things which at the moment they think of little or no Consequence.

   In a letter to a friend, Stephen wrote:

   > My friends at times tell me I have too much patience and forbearance, but I think not, for without these I never should have succeeded in my colonization of Texas.

3. Stephen Austin is now buried in the State Cemetery in Austin, Texas. The graves of Moses Austin and his wife, Maria, remain in the city cemetery of Potosi, Missouri.

4. After Mirabeau Lamar became the second president of the Republic of Texas, he found a beautiful hill that rose from the banks of the Colorado River in South-Central Texas. He chose it to be the site for the capital of the Republic. It was named to honor the work and dedication of a father and his son ...MOSES and STEPHEN F. AUSTIN

ABOUT THE AUTHOR

Betsy Warren has an art education degree from Miami University in Ohio and attended the Chicago Art Institute. She has written and illustrated many books for children. Most of them are about her favorite subject, Texas. Her works of historical nonfiction include *Twenty Texans, Indians Who Lived in Texas, Wilderness Walkers, Explorers in Early Texas,* and a *Let's Remember* series of five books about the people and events in Texas history. She also writes for magazines and works as a musician. Mrs. Warren lives in Austin, Texas.

PICTURE CREDITS

Amon Carter Museum, Fort Worth: pp. 28t (after John Woodhouse Audubon, *Lepus Texianus, Aud. and Bach. Texian Hare, Male. Natural Size.* 1848, lithograph, 1965.101), 33 (A.A. Parker, *Trip to the West and Texas,* Library Collection), 42 (Frederic S. Remington, *Drum Corps, Mexican Army,* 1889, oil on panel, 1961.239)

Austin History Center, Austin Public Library: pp. 29b, 30b, 44, 45, 51

The Center for American History, The University of Texas at Austin: pp. vi, 23, 34, 35b, 36, 43

The Connecticut Historical Society, Hartford, Connecticut: p. 14 (detail)

From the collections of the Dallas Historical Society: p. 26

Department of the Treasury, Bureau of Engraving and Printing: p. 3tb

Harry Ransom Humanities Research Center, The University of Texas at Austin: pp. 16, 39

Maryland Historical Society, Baltimore: p. 4b (detail)

Muséum d'Histoire Naturelle-Le Havre, no. 62052 and no. 62070: pp. 11, 18

State Historical Society of Missouri, Columbia: pp. 6, 7 (detail), 10t (detail), 12b (detail of *Osage Hunters,* Irving E. Couse mural, Missouri State Capitol)

Courtesy of the Texas Memorial Museum, The University of Texas at Austin: pp. 2b, 13b, 35t

Archives Division-Texas State Library: pp. 29t, 37, 46b

West Virginia Department of Commerce: p. 8b

Public domain: pp. 3ta (reproduction courtesy the Library of Congress), 9 (reproduction courtesy the Library of Congress), 10b and 19 (from Schoolcraft, *Lead Mines of Missouri*), 25 (reproduction courtesy the Library of Congress), 28b (reproduction courtesy Archives Division-Texas State Library), 31 (reproduction courtesy the Center for American History, The University of Texas at Austin)

All other illustrations produced and provided by the author.

BIBLIOGRAPHY

Barker, Eugene C. *The Life of Stephen F. Austin: Founder of Texas, 1793-1836.* Austin: Texas State Historical Association, 1949. Lamar & Barton, 1925.

Gracy II, David B. *Moses Austin: His Life.* San Antonio: Trinity University Press, 1987.

Hoff, Carol. *Wilderness Pioneer: Stephen F. Austin of Texas.* Dallas: Hendrick-Long Publishing Co., 1987

Texas State Historical Association. *The Handbook of Texas.* 2 vols. Austin: Texas State Historical Association, 1952.

Texas State Historical Association. *The Handbook of Texas.* A Supplement. Austin: Texas State Historical Association, 1976.

INDEX